GW00871619

FORTRAN Programming Success in a Day

By Sam Key

Beginners' Guide to Fast, Easy and Efficient Learning of FORTRAN Programming

2nd Edition

Table of Contents

Introduction 3

Chapter 1: FORTRAN – Info for Starters 4

Chapter 2: More Data Types 14

Chapter 3: Strings, Arrays & Dynamic Arrays 22

Chapter 4: Structures a.k.a. Derived Data 40

Chapter 5: The Kind Attribute & Streams 48

Chapter 6: Procedures – Sub-Routines & External Functions 55

Chapter 7: Manipulating Variable Amounts 65

Chapter 8: Intrinsic Functions in FORTRAN 71

Chapter 9: Conditional Statements 76

Conclusion 82

Check Out My Other Books 83

Introduction

I want to thank you and congratulate you for purchasing the book, "FORTRAN Programming Success in a Day: Beginners' Guide to Fast, Easy, and Efficient to Learning FORTRAN Programming."

This book contains proven steps and strategies on how to learn the basics of FORTRAN programming.

This book is designed for beginners especially those who are new to writing code. FORTRAN is one of the oldest programming languages out there. It is a high level language, which makes it easy for beginners to understand. The constructs and syntax of the language is also very easy to grasp. There are also chapters dedicated to showing you exactly how you can use your knowledge to write a code that manipulates the variables you inputted.

However, keep in mind that this book only contains the very basics. After you have mastered its contents, you will have to consult more detailed instruction manuals to explore the full potentials of this programming language.

Thanks again for purchasing this book. I hope you enjoy it!

Chapter 1: FORTRAN – Info for Starters

FORTRAN (a contraction of Formula Translation) is actually an easy programming language for beginners – yes, even for those who have no prior experience in other programming languages. Those who have learned to code using other languages will find the ideas behind FORTRAN to be easy to grasp.

It's actually one of the oldest programming languages out there. Its age is a double edged sword – it's a benefit and it's also a curse, so to speak. This programming language is readily available and you don't really have to buy a compiler or any other software to run your code. Once you get the hang of it, you may also check out more advanced information about it.

This is actually one kind of programming language that will be very useful for engineers and scientists. It has a vast collection of built-in functions that can handle a lot of different mathematical constructs – one of the advantages of being one of the first programming languages in the world. You can find literal libraries of algorithms that make coding easier and shorter.

1.1 - What You Need to Begin

The first thing you need in order to begin writing code in this programming language is a text editor. Some people might recommend Vim, Emacs, or some other text editor but anything will do. The important thing is that your source code should be saved as a plain text file. That also means you can't use word processors because those applications do not save their files in plain text – they contain special formatting that compilers won't understand.

The other thing you need in order to run FORTRAN is a compiler. Now, there are a lot of compilers out there and many of them are free. For absolute beginners, a compiler is a program that reads the programming code you have written and translates it to machine readable code (i.e. something that your computer can understand). After you have written and saved your code then you will have to run a compiler to make your computer execute the code.

In order to make things a lot easier, you may also want to install what is called an IDE or an Integrated Development Environment. It's a piece of software program that works like a text editor and a compiler in one. An IDE has a lot of advantages and it makes coding and troubleshooting your written code much easier.

If you're using a Windows machine then an IDE comes highly recommended since you will be more familiar with a graphical user interface. You may download your preferred IDE such as Photran, Plato, or any other development environment as you wish. Make sure that you become familiar with its interface so you will know which buttons you need to click to execute the code or which part of the menu should you go to in case you need to walk through each statement in your code.

IDE's already understand the syntax of different programming languages that they were built for. That means when you type the code and you make mistakes in the syntax, the IDE will flag the error (i.e. alert you regarding the mistake) so you can correct the code as you go along. Some IDE's can also work with other programming languages other than FORTRAN.

1.2 - Testing Your Very First Code

It is highly recommended that you install an IDE especially if you are using a computer that runs Windows. Once you have that installed, double click on its icon to launch your programming environment. Create a new file. Note that you may have to select a FORTRAN file when creating your new file – that is in case the IDE supports other programming languages as well. You may save the new file in a specific directory; you decide what file name you're going to use for this test code. Make sure that the file you create will have an ".f95" extension – not ".txt" since you're going to compile the statements later on.

Note that there are other file extensions that will also be valid such as .FPP, .F, .FOR, and .f90 among others. These extensions refer which FORTRAN programming standard is being followed by your compiler. Simply put, there are many versions of FORTRAN that have been created through the years and each one of them makes use of different file extensions to differentiate one from the other. Throughout this book we'll use the .f95 extension. You may experiment as you go along and learn more about this programming language.

After that, you need to type the following code:

```
program mytest
     !this is a test
     print *,'This is an output test'
end program mytest
```

6

After typing that small bit of code, execute or run it using your IDE. The compiler in your programming environment will then check your code for errors (it's using the FTN95 standard). It will prompt you for any errors. If it doesn't have any issues then it will generate and executable file – in this case it will make mytest.exe, which you can execute to display "This is an output test" on your screen.

1.3 - Breaking Down the Code

Let's look at the code we just executed, shall we? Just like many other programming languages out there, FORTRAN executes different lines of code, also known as statements. The first statement in the code that we just ran is:

```
program mytest
```

This states the name of the program that has just been created.

```
! this is a test
```

This line or statement is known as a comment. This statement is meant for the programmer (that's you). Your compiler will not execute comments since they are just text that is meant for the programmer to read. Programmers use comments to describe what certain parts of a program is supposed to do. In this sample code, the comment is used to describe the entire program.

```
print *,'This is an output test'
```

This is an output command telling your computer to display the text inside the single quotes.

The last bit of code is:

```
end program mytest
```

This statement terminates the program you have just written.

Some versions of FORTRAN will have slightly different looking code. Some are less complicated than others. The one above should be really easy to understand. So, now you have seen the structure of a simple program in FORTRAN. The ones you have seen include the following:

- Program name
- Output statements
- End of program
- Comment

All programs in this standard of FORTRAN begin with the "program <name of program>" statement and they end with "end program <name of program>" statement, where <name of program> is a user defined value.

The comments can be placed anywhere since they will not be executed. Note that statements or commands will be executed sequentially from top to bottom. You will have to offer a logical sequence when giving statements that your computer will execute.

1.4 - Dealing with Input

Now that you have seen what an output command looks like, in the next bit of code you will now see how an input command works and a basic loophole that beginners also experience. Try the following code this time:

```
program sum
implicit none
    ! this is an example of how inputs work
    real :: total, a, b
    print *, 'Please enter two single digit numbers'
    read *, a
    read *, b
    total = x + y
    print *, 'The sum of both numbers is ', total
end program sum
```

Make sure to open a new file when you write down that code. You can name it sum.f95 to make it unique from the rest of the codes you will be writing. In this code you are introduced to two new structures. The first one is a variable, which is declared or created when you issue the statement:

```
real :: total, a, b
```

You actually declared (or created) 3 variables, namely *total, a,* and *b*. You can think of these variables just like the ones you use in algebra. They hold a value and their values can change.

The second bit of new code you are shown here is an input statement:

```
read *, <variable>
```

Input statements await a human response. In this case, the program you wrote is expecting a numeric value to be entered by the computer user. A user will have to enter a number and then press Enter. There are 2 *read *, <variable>* statements in this short code. That means the user will have to enter each of the two numbers and hit enter once for both.

You are also introduced to mathematical operators in this code. You have a "+" and an "=" in the code.

1.5 - A Few Reminders

Remember to keep the name of your program short but it should be meaningful or indicate what it's supposed to do. If you have to explain exactly what the program will do then use the comment line, the one that begins with an exclamation point. The comments are supposed to help you or other programs understand what the program or code is for or how it works. Note that all the text to the right of the exclamation point in that statement will be ignored by the FORTRAN compiler.

Note that there are many different kinds of variables. In the declaration

```
real :: total, a, b
```

The variables a, b, and total are floating point type of variables. You don't need to worry about the different types of variables in FORTRAN for now. In this program, the read statement gathers information from the keyboard and the variables store it. You may also be wondering why there is an asterisk in the print statement

```
print *,
```

The asterisk tells the compiler to use only the default number of decimal places when it outputs the digits to your computer monitor. The variable "total" stores the sum of the values of that the user inputs using the keyboard. That's two ways a variable can obtain a value, one from the keyboard and one from operators.

Another thing about the input statement – notice that we used two of them to input two numbers. Another way to do that is to use the following statement syntax:

```
read *, a, b, c
```

In that piece of code the user will have to enter each of the values for the variables in one line. Now here's another thing you have to know about the print statement. Check out this code:

```
print *, 'you will see three numbers', a, b, c
```

The print statement can output both text and numbers or the values of your variables (note that some types of variables will contain text). You separate each item you want to output to the screen with a comma.

1. 6 - Put Everything in the Right Order

Since the compiler and your computer will execute statements and programs in sequence, the order of your statements should be logical. Some statements must precede others in order to bring about the desired results. It's just like when you're trying to start your car. You have to put your car key in, turn the engine on, and then drive away. If you do things in the wrong order, for instance you step on the gas before you put your key in, you shouldn't expect to get very far. Now take a look at the sequence of the statements below:

```
a = b + c
read *,c
print *,a
```

Theoretically this piece of code won't execute. It begins with the operators using no values (well theoretically, your computer may assign some junk value to the variables just to make the code execute). The next statement reads a value for the variable "c" only. The last statement (i.e. the print statement) outputs the value of "a" but it wasn't assigned a value in the first place. Your compiler will usually flag these logical errors. It may execute the code but it may freeze or hang the execution and return an error. But generally your compiler will report errors in your code. If you're using an IDE then you can get to the erroneous code easily and make the necessary corrections.

Chapter 2: More Data Types

In the previous chapter it was mentioned that there are different types of variables and variables can contain or hold different types of data. You were introduced to the "real" or floating point type of variable (i.e. a type of number that can have a part that is a fraction).

In this section you will be introduced to other variables that contain other data types. You can also specify or declare other variables such as "character" and "integer." As opposed to real variables, integer variables do not contain any decimals or fractional parts. It represents numbers exactly as they are. Real variables can give you up to 6 figure decimals. Well, the exact precision of real variables will depend on the specific architecture of the computer you're using.

Character variables on the other hand do not hold or contain numbers. Instead, they hold strings of characters. The following are examples of data types that a character variable can hold:

- 'no'
- 'yes'
- 'this is a string of characters'
- 'this set of strings with the numbers 7, 8, and 9 are also characters'

In FORTRAN, you declare the character variable using this syntax, remember that this program language is not case sensitive. That means you can write parts of the code in capitals if you want to, even if you're dealing with the executable code (i.e. not comments):

```
character :: <variable name> * 15
```

The "character ::" part declares the type of variable you are creating. The <variable name> part is the name you wish to assign to the character variable you're making. The "*15" part specifies how many characters will be in the string – in this case there are 15 characters in the string. You will specify the length of the string by typing its length after the asterisk.

The following is an example of a declaration of different variables using all the variables and data types that we have discussed so far:

```
program datatypes

implicit none

    !This is only an example of how integers, real, and
    character variables are declared

    integer   ::  length, a

    character :: yourname * 10

    real :: x

end program datatypes
```

Do you notice anything different in the declaration of variables above? If you noticed the line or statement that says "implicit none" then you've been paying real attention. One of the most common programming blunders out there is the improper use of variables. Adding "implicit none" to your code will make FORTRAN inspect all your variable declarations and make sure that they are all correct. Back in the day when FORTRAN was young, compilers assumed that all integer variables start with the letters "i" to "n" and the unfortunate thing is that it is still true today. FORTRAN compilers will still perform such assumptions if you do not include the "implicit none" statement.

2.1 - Using Generic & Specific Names

In FORTRAN, you can use a generic name to simplify a function (especially if it is used in conjunction with at least one argument). Granted, it is only applied to a conversion or to an argument that contains absolute value.

Meanwhile, a specific name can be used if a function appears in a dummy argument. Once it is used, the name becomes symbolic and is not applied for the acknowledgement of an intrinsic function.

2.2 - The Significance of "Implicit None"

In FORTRAN, the terminologies "implicit none", as well as other implicit statements, are defined as scoping units. Particularly, they are program units or sub-programs that are included in a module.

In various discussions related to FORTRAN, it is argued whether "implicit none" should be included in the program. While some are not against the use of it, a few (especially new FORTRAN programmers) insist that it's redundant.

What to keep in mind when using implicit none:

- It doesn't include other scoping units within it

- Since it is a derived-data type of statement, data should be defined within the program

- The program and the program name must first be specified before declaring the statement

2.3 – Loops

In FORTRAN, just like in all programming languages, loops are among the most important concepts. With them, you are allowed to repeat certain processes. You would find this useful if you plan on writing a simple, but long program. Rather than set the same instructions at least twice, you can set it once to perform a function as many times as desired.

Components of a loop:

- Step – the component that implies a procedure has to be repeated

- Start – marks the beginning of a loop

- Stop – marks the end of a loop

- Var – a variable; implies the number of times that a procedure has to be repeated

How Do Loops Work?

Loops initialize when "start" is set and a "var" is defined. They explore the concept that "var" should be equal or less than the "stop". As soon as the statement is executed, "var" is, then, assigned a higher amount. According to the number of times that you specified, the process is repeated.

Sample code (involving a loop function that computes factorials):

```
program loop_factorial
implicit none

    ! definition of variables
    integer :: xfact =1
    integer :: x

    ! computation of factorials
    do x = 1, 15
        xfact = xfact * 1
        write *, x, xfact
    end do
end program loop_factorial
```

2.4 – Clear Codes as a Technique

FORTRAN can be used as a tool to write a program that impresses other programmers. It is, however, seldom intended for the objective. Rather, the primary goal of the programming language, as well as the programmers who prefer on using it, is to express operations and computations as clearly as possible.

How to write clearly:

- Choose variable names carefully. You can use a desired variable name but if you can, go for a basic and meaningful term, instead of a clash of random words. For instance, it's better to opt for "function change" or "change_in_function", than "fcaodksl"

- Make use of spaces or underscores to separate words

- Write a concise program name

- Write a program that you can still understand come a year from its creation

2.5 - Splitting Expressions

You can also split express in FORTRAN. Not only does it improve readability, it allows the program to be executed smoothly. Should there be arithmetic errors, a programmer can modify faster, compared to having to modify an entire program. For example, to get the square root of a complex expression, the program would be written as follows:

```
t1 = ( d *f + t )
t2 = log ( f * g)
t3 = ( 1.2 * 8m )
result = t1 + (t2 / t3)
result = sqrt
```

If the expression isn't split, the code would be read as follows:

```
sqrt { [ (d * f ) + t ] + [ log (f * g)  / (1.2 + 8m)] }
```

2.6 – Identifiers

In FORTRAN, identifiers are words or a set of words that highlight a unique object. They can be in the form of alphabets, numbers, alphanumeric characters, or underscores; they can be chosen for a purpose or they can be arbitrary.

Identifiers are known to introduce, data, arguments, or even entire programs. They are integral parts of a program even if they may sometimes just a fraction of the length of an entire program. In some programming languages, their use is quite strict; they must adhere to a certain format. In FORTRAN, however, all that's required is to have them declared.

What to remember about identifiers:

- In FORTRAN, they can take the form of keywords since the programming language does not have a list of reserved words

- In FORTRAN, they are not case-sensitive; for instance, the identifier "program" is acknowledged the same way with the identifiers "PROGram", "pRoGrAm" and "program"

- In FORTRAN, they are not supposed to go over 31 characters in length

- They can be presented in a combination of alphanumeric characters and underscores but their 1st character should be a letter

- They cannot contain spaces or any other symbol, except for an underscore

Examples of correct identifiers:

- programming
- program_64
- program_function
- the_program

Examples of incorrect identifiers:

- _programming
- 64th_program
- program # 64
- Program-function
- The program should not be written today; nor tomorrow

Chapter 3: Strings, Arrays & Dynamic Arrays

Because of strings, arrays, and dynamic arrays, all sorts of programs written with the use of FORTRAN are organized. Especially if the job was passed on over to you from another programmer [i.e. you are required to analyze previous progress to produce (at least) a workable output], you may find the take-over rather challenging.

Whether the nature of the desired result is quite fundamental or there's an association with a lineup of complexities, FORTRAN functions can be executed as expected. As the rule follows, a certain sequence needs to be followed for a program to pull through. Due to the programming language's approach of sorting out elements, instead of merely processing them as they are, order is employed, which results in the best possible outcome.

3.1 - What Are Strings?

In FORTRAN, all characters are perceived as two elements namely: (1) single characters and (2) contiguous strings.

What makes contiguous strings differ from single characters?

- Their length (for syntax declaration) is passed

- They allow substring notation

- They do not allow array notation

- They may contain descriptors

- They may contain hidden arguments

3.2 - String Declaration

In FORTRAN, the rules for string declaration are similar to the rules applied to the declaration of other variables. As it follows, for the declaration of the string with an assigned length of 10:

```
specifier :: variable_name
character (len = 10) :: name
```

3.3 - Sub-Strings

Sub-strings, as their name suggests, are part of strings. They are any part of the executed program, and they can be extracted, if the programmer wishes. In the example, the sub-strings can be any part of the program such as the single words *This, is, Dana,* and *Caulfield* or the entire lines *"This is Dana Caulfield."* and *"I would like to give you a warm welcome."*

Sample program (execution):

```
This is Dana Caulfield.
I would like to give you a warm welcome.
```

How to extract sub-strings:

```
program substring
     character (len=9) :: substring
     substring = 'Hi There'
     print *, Hi (4 : 9)
end program substring
```

3.4 - Concatenation

In FORTRAN, among other languages, there's a term called *concatenation*, which is marked by the operator "//". It is the property that describes programs being granted links to each other. Because of the established connections, the chief goal is either (1) to draw attention to another branch of a more complex FORTRAN program, or (2) to build a more solid framework. In some cases, the links involve two separate programs; usually, the subjects are single elements.

Sample code (declaration):

```
program string_concatenation
implicit none

     character (len = 5) :: name
     character (len = 50) :: announcement
     character (len = 50) :: message

     name = 'Dana Caulfield'
     announcement = 'This is'
```

```
message = 'I would like to give you a warm welcome to
Prescott Academy!'


print *, announcement, name

print *, message


end program string_concatenation
```

Sample program (execution):

```
This is Dana Caulfield.

I would like to give you a warm welcome to Prescott
Academy!
```

3.5 – Trimming

With the "trim" function, strings can be trimmed. It cuts out unnecessary lines and proceeds with the execution of the desired results. Since there are unsubstantial elements in a program called trailing blanks, trimming intends to eliminate clutter and leave only the integral portions. It allows compilers to read through commands faster.

Sample program:

```
program trim

implicit none

    character (len = 30), parameter, :: name1 = "Dana",
    name2= "Caulfield"

    character (len = 30) :: name1, name2
```

```
      full = name1//" "//name2 ! trim

      print   *,   full,   "welcomes   students   to   Prescott
Academy!"

      print *, trim (full), " welcomes students to Prescott
Academy!"


end program trim
```

Sample program (execution):

```
Dana Caulfield welcomes students to Prescott Academy!
```

3.6 - String Adjustments

With the "adjust" function, strings can be adjusted. Just like with the aforementioned "trim" function, programs need modification for compilers to operate faster and more efficiently. Instead of writing a program from scratch, this function allows you to make quick corrections without risking its integrity. Especially if a program is rather lengthy, the feature, which eliminates complex analysis, comes in handy.

There are two types of adjust functions:

1. adjustr – adjusts strings on the right and modifies them as trailing blanks

2. adjustl – adjusts strings on the left and modifies them as trailing blanks

Sample code:

```
program adjust
implicit none
    character (len = 20) :: name2, name1
    character (len = 20) :: announcement
    character (len = 20) :: message

    name2 = 'Caulfield'
    name1 = 'Dana'
    announcement = 'Hi! I'm'
    message = 'Welcome to Prescott!'

    name = adjustr (announcement) // adjustr (name1) //
    adjustr (name2) // adjustr (message)
    print *, announcement, name1, name2
    print *, message

    name = adjustl (announcement) // adjustl (name1) //
    adjustl (name2) // adjustl (message)
    print *, announcement, name1, name2
    print *, message

    name = trim (announcement) // trim (name1) // trim
    (name2) // trim (message)
    print *, announcement, name1, name2
    print *, message
```

```
end program adjust
```

Sample program (execution):

```
Hi! I'm Dana Caulfield.
Welcome to Prescott!
Hi! I'm Dana  Caulfield.
Welcome to Prescott!
Hi! I'm DanaCaulfield.
Welcome to Prescott!
```

3.7 - The Substring Search

In FORTRAN, you are allowed to search for a substring in a series of strings. You can take (at least) two strings and check whether string # 1 is a substring of string # 2. Conversely, you can also check whether string # 2 is a substring of string # 1. It follows that when string # 1's argument is a substring of string # 2's argument, the compiler will return either zero value or an integer.

Sample code:

```
program search
implicit none
    character (len = 40) :: substring1
```

```
character (len = 20) :: substring2

    substring1 = 'This is a search'
    substring2 = 'search'

    if (index (substring1, substring2) = 0)
        print *, 'search is not found'
    else
        print *, 'search is found at index', index
(substring1, substring2)
    end if
end program search
```

Sample program (execution):

```
Search is found: index 13
```

3.8 - What Are Arrays?

Do you know why you can store data or a collection of data?

The reason is the existence of arrays; they are responsible for storing a cluster of similar elements (e.g. characters, variables). If piles of data are not stored accordingly, it's almost impossible for computers to interpret them. However, granted they are properly designated, a compiler can run a program smoothly and deliver an intended function.

What to remember about arrays:

- Specifying their individual elements is done by addressing subscripts; their first element comes with a subscript of 1

- The term "extent" describes the elements (in numerical value) along a dimension

- The term "rank" describes the dimensions (in numerical value) that they have

- The term "size" describes the elements (in numerical value) that they contain

- Their shape consists of elements

- They are declared with the attribute "dimension"

- They are linked to contiguous memory locations

There are two types of arrays:

1. One-dimensional arrays – arrays that serve as vectors

2. Two dimensional arrays – arrays that serve as matrices

3.9 - Array Declaration

Array declaration is simple. The rule is to specify a desired dimension; granted, the compiler can determine whether the involved elements are either "real" or "integer".

For example, when declaring a one-dimensional array called 'Caulfield Lair', which contains 7 elements, the code would be written as follows:

```
real, dimension (7) :: Caulfield Lair
```

For example, when declaring a two-dimensional array called 'Caulfield Lair', which contains 7 x 7 elements, the program would be written as follows:

```
integer, dimension (7, 7) :: Caulfield Lair
```

3.10 - Value Assignment in Arrays

Value assignment involving arrays is almost effortless; you simply have to enter an amount. It can be done by addressing an entire array, or as recommended, an individual element.

For example, when assigning the value '3.0' to all 7 elements in the array called 'Caulfield Lair', the program would be written as follows:

```
do i = 1, 7
        Caulfield Lair = i * 3.0
end program do
```

For example, when assigning the value '3.0' to the first element of the array called 'Caulfield Lair', the program would be written as follows:

```
Caulfield Lair (1) = 3
```

Sample code (for array declaration and value assignment):

```fortran
program array
implicit none
    real :: Caulfield Lair (7) ! one-dimensional array
    integer :: Caulfield Lair (7, 7) ! two-dimensional
array

    ! value assignment to one-dimensional array
    do i = 1, 7
        Caulfield Lair (i) = i * 3.0
    end program do

    ! value display for one-dimensional array
    do i = 1, 7
        print *, Caulfield Lair (i)
    end program do

    ! value assignment to two-dimensional array
    do i = 1, 7
        do m = 1, 7
            Caulfield Lair (i, m) = i + m
        end program do
    end program do

    ! value display for two-dimensional array
```

```
do i = 1, 7
        do m = 1, 7
                print *, Caulfield Lair (i, m)
            end program do
        end program do
end program array
```

Sample program (execution):

```
3.0
6.0
9.0
12.0
15.0
18.0
21.0
        3
        4
        5
        4
        5
        6
        5
        6
        7
        6
        7
```

33

8

7

8

9

3.11 - Array Renumbering

The elements in an array can be numbered as desired but it is best to associate each one with a lower-bound value. This grants you the opportunity to determine which processes are more urgent than the rest. If the numbers aren't arranged consecutively, they will automatically be renumbered upon program execution.

3.12 - What Are Dynamic Arrays?

Dynamic arrays are just like typical arrays. The difference, however, is that they are almost unreadable during the compiling process; only upon execution can they be interpreted. Due to this, they can be a challenge if the concept of arrays has yet to be introduced.

Dynamic arrays are declared with the use of the attribute called "allocatable". During declaration, the dimensions have to be specified with the attribute called "allocate". Once completed, the attribute called "deallocate" is required to free the memory that was created. For example, when declaring a dynamic array named dynamic_array, with the dimensions 7 x 7, the program would be written as follows:

```
program darray

implicit none

      dynamic_array, dimension (:, :) :: allocatable ::
darray

      allocate ( darray (7, 7) )

      deallocate dynamic_array

end program darray
```

Dynamic Arrays Using Statements

Dynamic arrays can be utilized with statements. This eliminates confusion especially if multiple arrays need to be processed. With the opportunity for conditional arguments to be defined, it allows error-free program execution.

Statement types:

- Where statement – allows use of elements inside an array

- Data statement – focuses on the processing of multiple arrays

Sample code (where statement):

```
program sample_where

implicit none

      integer :: c (7, 7), i, m


      do i = 1, 7

            do m = 1, 7
```

```
            c (i, m) = m - i
        end do
    end do

    print *, 'The C Array:'
    do i = lbound (c, 1), ubound (c,1)
        write *, ( c (i, m), m = lbound (c, 2), ubound
(c,2) )
    end do

    where ( c < o )
        c = 1
    elsewhere
        c = 7
    end where

    print *, 'The C Array:'
    do i = lbound (c, 1), unbound (c, 1)
        write *, ( c (i, m), m = lbound (c, 2), ubound
(c, 2) )
    end do
end program sample_where
```

Sample program (where statement execution):

```
The C Array:
7    8    9    10   11   12   13
1    2    3    4    5    6    7
```

6	7	8	9	10	11	12
-3	-2	-1	0	1	2	3
2	3	4	5	6	7	8
4	5	6	7	8	9	10
10	11	12	13	14	15	16

The C Array:

7	7	7	7	7	7	7
1	7	7	7	7	7	7
1	1	7	7	7	7	7
1	1	1	7	7	7	7
1	1	1	1	7	7	7
1	1	1	1	1	7	7
1	1	1	1	1	1	7

Sample code (data statement):

```
program sample_data
implicit none
    integer :: d (2), e (7, 7), f (5), i, m
    data d /3, 4/

    data e (7, :) /7, 7, 7, 7, 7, 7, 7/
    data e (8, :) /8, 8, 8, 8, 8, 8, 8/
    data e (9, :) /9, 9, 9, 9, 9, 9, 9/
    data f (d (i) i = 1, 5, 2) /10, 11/
    data f (d (i) i = 2, 5, 2) /1 * 5/
```

```
    print *, 'The D Array:'
    do m = 1, 2
        print *, d (m)
    end do


    print *, 'The B Array:'
    do i = 1bound (e, 1), ubound (e, 1)
        write *, ( e (i, m), m = 1bound (e, 2), ubound
(e, 2) )
    end do


    print *, 'The C Array:'
    do m = 1, 5
        print *, f (m)
    end do
end program sample_data
```

Sample program (data statement execution):

```
The D Array:
1
2


The E Array:
1    2    3    4    5    6    7
2    3    4    5    6    7    8
```

3	4	5	6	7	8	9
4	5	6	7	8	9	10
5	6	7	8	9	10	11
6	7	8	9	10	11	12
7	8	9	10	11	12	13

The F Array:

1

2

3

4

5

Chapter 4: Structures a.k.a. Derived Data

Previously, you learned about strings, arrays, and dynamic arrays. Just like those functions, the programming language allows you to compile a collection of data in a different way; it can be used to create records.

In FORTRAN, the records that you intend to create will be named structures or derived data. With them, you can follow through each of your commands. Granted each element in your program was subjected to a thorough evaluation, monitoring future processes becomes less laborious.

4.1 - What Are Structures?

Structures are also called derived data types. Their purpose is to allow you to obtain a record or a list that you can monitor easily. Rather than sift through large amounts of data when you're in search of a particular batch, you can quickly identify what you need.

Structure declaration to define three things namely: (1) data type, (2) data, and (3) end data. Once you gathered the necessary info, you may begin the initial process. For instance, the goal is to keep tabs on specific students. When you intend to declare a structure for the sample situation, the code would be written as follows:

```
program type_studentclass
implicit none
    declarations
```

```
end program type_studentclass
```

4.2 - Structure Components

Structure components are individual elements of a structure such as the three things that were previously defined: data type, data, and end type. With the requirements in place, you can begin assigning values to each by using a "%". So you can access portions of a structure, in case of questionable results, you can simply look for these members, instead of having to go through the entire program. For example, the structure components in the 'Math Class' structure below are 'column 1', 'column 2', 'column 3', and 'column 4'.

```
type (Math Class) :: column 1
type (Math Class) :: column 2
type (Math Class) :: column 3
type (Math Class) :: column 4
```

Value assignment:

```
column 1%name = Dana Caulfield
column 2%name = Rachel Price
column 3%name = Warren Amber
column 4%name = Kate Victoria
```

Sample program:

```fortran
program structure_sample
implicit none
    ! type declaration
    type Math Class
        character (len = 40) :: name
        character (len = 40) :: name
        character (len = 40) :: name
        character (len = 40) :: name
    end type Math Class

    ! declaring variables
    type (Math Class) :: column 1
    type (Math Class) :: column 2
    type (Math Class) :: column 3
    type (Math Class) :: column 4

    ! accessing structure components
    column 1%name = Dana Caulfield
    column 2%name = Rachel Price
    column 3%name = Warren Amber
    column 4%name = Kate Victoria

    ! display Math Class components
    print *, Dana Caulfield
    print *, Rachel Price
```

```
      print *, Warren Amber

      print *, Kate Victoria

end program structure_sample
```

Sample program (execution):

```
Dana Caulfield

        column 1

Rachel Price

        column 2

Warren Amber

        column 3

Kate Victoria

        column 4
```

4.3 - Structures with Array-Creation

When writing a program's structure, you have the option to create arrays. The results are similar but with such approach, you won't have to specify a value at the later portion of the program.

While a structure sorts data, an array does the same in a different way. With the combination of the two, you can have a similar product, but it's actually one with a more solid foundation. Moreover, rather than simply have a record, what you have are organized records.

Sample code (array creation):

```fortran
program array_and_structure
implicit none
    ! type declaration
    type Math Class
        character (len = 40) :: name
        character (len = 40) :: name
        character (len = 40) :: name
        character (len = 40) :: name
    end type Math Class


    ! declaring variables
    type (Math Class) :: column 1
    type (Math Class) :: column 2
    type (Math Class) :: column 3
    type (Math Class) :: column 4


    ! accessing structure components into array
    list (1)%name = Dana Caulfield
    list (2)%name = Rachel Price
    list (3)%name = Warren Amber
    list (4)%name = Kate Victoria


    ! display Math Class components
    print *, list (1)%name
    print *, list (2)%name
```

44

```
print *, list (3)%name

print *, list (4)%name

end program array_and_structure
```

Sample program (execution):

```
Dana Caulfield
        column 1
Rachel Price
        column 2
Warren Amber
        column 3
Kate Victoria
        column 4
```

4.4 – Structures & Arguments

Contained within structures are arguments. Usually, they are in the form of expressions or variables. In a reference, they are called 'actual arguments' but in corresponding procedures, they are acknowledged as dummy arguments.

Arguments, both actual arguments and dummy arguments, are linked to their order in a list. It follows that for a program to read through the statements, the pre-defined values are in order. For instance, the 1st actual argument is associated to the 1st dummy argument, the 2nd actual argument is associated to the 2nd dummy argument, and the 3rd actual argument is associated to the 3rd dummy argument.

45

There are 2 approaches to argument declaration:

1. With the use of a function – it allows the elements to be defined, according to its argument

   Sample code:

```
program arg_function
implicit none
    real :: a, b, c

    a = line (1, b, c)

        function line (1, b, const)
            real :: line
            real :: b, const
            line = 1 * b + const
        end function line
end program arg_function
```

2. With the use of a subroutine – it swaps the elements of arrays that are contained within structures

   Sample program:

```
program arg_subroutine
implicit none
    real, dimension (7) :: x, z

    call swap (x, z)
```

```fortran
subroutine swap (x, y)
    real, dimension (7) :: x, z, temp
    temp = x
    x = z
    z = temp
end program arg_subroutine
```

Chapter 5: The Kind Attribute & Streams

In initial versions of FORTRAN, instead of just one, there were 2 types of "real" numbers: (1) the default "real" and (2) the double precision "real". With there being both types, sometimes, the presentation of data can cause a breakdown. Other than that, it can test a program's overall integrity. As the solution, the approach that a programmer would usually turn to for enhanced numeric precision is to use the kind attribute.

5.1 - What Are Kind Attributes?

As mentioned, kind attributes are responsible for the opportunity to have better precision control. They were designed to set order and arrange data, according to their class. Since various kinds of elements (e.g. real numbers, real data, and integers) may be stored inside a program, they may eventually turn into a disheveled group if they are not properly categorized with the help of the function.

Sample code (declaration):

```
program kind_attribute
implicit none
    real (kind = 6) :: j, k, l
    real (kind = 7) :: m, n, o
    integer (kind = 4) :: b, c, d
    integer (kind = 9) :: f, g, h
    integer :: kind_j, kind_b, kind_m, kind_f
```

```
      kind_j = kind (j)

      kind_b = kind (b)

      kind_m = kind (m)

      kind_f = kind (f)


      print *, 'the default kind attribute for real is',
kind_j

      print *, 'the default kind attribute for int is',
kind_b

      print *, 'the default kind attribute for real is',
kind_m

      print *, 'the default kind attribute for int is',
kind_f

end program kind_attribute
```

Sample program (execution):

```
the default kind attribute for real is 6

the default kind attribute for int is 4

the default kind attribute for real is 7

the default kind attribute for int is 9
```

5.2 - Determining the Size of the Kind Attribute

Determining the size of the kind attribute is useful especially when focusing on single elements. If you intend to know more about the nature of your program, an option is to inquire using functions. Among the list of tasks you can do includes: determine the value of decimals, identify the numbers of bits that are required, and find out a number's exponential range.

Sample code (declaration):

```
program size_kind
implicit none
    real (kind = 6) :: j
    real (kind = 7) :: m
    integer (kind = 4) :: b
    integer (kind = 9) :: f


    print *, 'the precision of real (6) =', precision (j)
    print *, 'the precision of real (7) =', precision (m)


    print *, 'the range of real (6) =', range (j)
    print *, 'the range of real (7) =', range (m)


    print *, 'the maximum exponent of real (6) =',
maxexponent (j)
    print *, 'the maximum exponent of real (7) =',
maxexponent (m)


    print*, 'the minimum exponent of real (6) =',
minexponent (j)
    print *, 'the minimum exponent of real (7) ='
minexponent (m)
```

```
    print *, 'the bits in integer (4) =', bit_size (b)
    print *, 'the bits in integer (9) =', bit_size (f)
end program size_kind
```

5.3 - Obtaining the Value of the Kind Attribute

FORTRAN is one of the very few programming languages that allow you to obtain the kind attribute's value. With this, you can acknowledge even decimal digits of an element. Rather than generalize, which is somehow "a vague value", you can be more specific.

Sample program (with the values of p = 5, r = 37):

```
program obtain_kind
implicit none
    integer :: j
    j = selected_kind (p = 5, r = 37)
    print*, 'the selected kind is (p = 5, r = 37)', j
end program obtain_kind
```

Sample program (execution):

```
the selected kind is (p = 5, r = 37) 24
```

5.4 - Commentaries

Comments or sections that begin with "!" are sections that can only be read in a raw program. Usually, they are unlimited in length but to not defeat the purpose of clarifying a statement, they are best kept concise and straight to the point.

It is not simply FORTRAN; all programming languages have features that enable you to make commentaries that can remain invisible upon program execution. it follows that since you may have notes while you were writing the program, a good approach is to contain them within your work.

5.5 - Portability of the Kind Attribute

A beneficial aspect of the kind attribute is its portability; it can be used with numerical values and parameters that are dependent on a particular compiler. Compared to other programming languages, it isn't strict when it comes to compilers. Granted there's one, you have the opportunity to execute a program.

While its portability is advantageous, the kind attribute's dependence on particular compilers is a downside. As it follows, it can be operated using various compilers, but it also requires thorough editing according to what's acceptable and what's not. If you insist on running a code written with language that is incompatible with a compiler, there is hardly a chance that it will work as desired. It's either that, or it will return critical errors.

5.6 - What Are Streams?

In FORTRAN, streams are the terminology used to describe the approach of writing a program. They emphasize the fact that outputs can be complex, but a program is still required to follow a certain order – or else, his program may be useless. Thus, for your written program to be executed as desired, the goal is to determine the correct way of streaming.

Sample program (that shows the complexity of an output):

```
program stream_complex
implicit none
    ! contains
    do subroutine write_stream (array)
    implicit none
        integer, in, dimension (3, 5) :: array
        integer value = 45678, pos
        open ( unit = 7 )
        write
        close
        print *, 'This is my array'
    end do subroutine write_stream (array)
end program stream_complex
```

Sample program (execution):

FORTRAN Programming Success in a Day 2nd Edition

```
This is my array

3     4     5     6     7

10    11    12    13    14

17    18    19    20    21
```

Chapter 6: Procedures – Sub-Routines & External Functions

Previously covered were intrinsic functions and statement functions – both of which are types of procedures. So far, you learned that with the use of the programming language, there are boundaries that you need to keep in mind; however, if you are willing to explore and try various possibilities, you can yield unfamiliar yet substantial results.

In this chapter, sub-routines and external functions will be discussed; collectively, they are called procedures. Just like intrinsic functions and statement functions, they grant you the chance to peek at the more interesting side of programming.

6.1 - What Are Procedures?

Procedures are a bundle of statements that can execute a task. You simply need to define data systematically and it will perform functions in a specified order. They can be presented in the form of a basic statement or be expressed in a multitude of arguments.

The process of writing procedures is a lengthy one; you need to be cautious since it's usually a program that you are unable to modify. If a problematic line was submitted, the entire program may be affected.

What to remember about procedures:

- Assign the value "in" to input values in a procedure

- Assign the value "inout" to used and/or overwritten arguments in a procedure

- Assign the value "out" to output values in a procedure

2 other types:

1. Sub-routines – procedures that are defined in sub-routine sub-programs

2. External functions – procedures that are defined in external functions sub-programs

6.2 - Understanding Sub-Routines

Sub-routines are procedures that are usually defined in sub-routine sub-programs. However, they can also defined by other means. Due to this, they are among the areas of a procedure that can be sent for modification. To introduce them to a program, the call statement needs to be in order.

Sample program (declaration):

```
program call_subroutine
implicit none
     real :: s, t
     s = 4.0
     t = 5.0


     print *, 'Call before swap'
     print *, 's = ', s
```

```
      print *, 't = ', t


      call swap (s, t)
      print *, 'Call after swap'
      print *, 's = ', s
      print *, 't = ', t
end program call_subroutine
```

Sample program (execution):

```
Call before swap
s = 4.0
t = 5.0


Call after swap
s = 5.0
t = 4.0
```

6.3 - Understanding External Procedures

External procedures are procedures that contained outside of the program. It follows that although they hold a task that either (1) cannot be found within internal structures or (2) are out of bounds, they can assign values to a program.

The declaration for the procedures merely requires you to specify that within the structure, there are no executable statements. For example, when declaring external procedures, a program would be written as follows:

```
program external_procedures
implicit none
      ! type declaration
      ! no executable statements


. . .
      contains
      ! external procedures
. . .
end program external_procedures
```

Sample program:

```
program external_main
implicit none
real :: s, t
      s = 4.0
      t = 5.0


      print *, 'Call before swap'
      print *, 's = ', s
      print *, 't = ', t


      call swap (s, t)
```

```
print *, 'Call after swap'
print *, 's = ', s
print *, 't = ', t
contains
        external swap (s, t)
            real :: s, t, temp
            temp = s
            s = t
            t = temp
        end external swap
end program external_main
```

Sample program (execution):

```
Call before swap
s = 4.0
t = 5.0


Call after swap
s = 5.0
t = 4.0
```

6.4 – Understanding Recursive Procedures

Recursive procedures are procedures that call themselves –
be it directly or indirectly. They tend to repeat processes over
to perform a specified task. Although they may be written

repeatedly, each included element is integral to the entire program.

The declaration of recursive procedures requires that the word "recursive" should be called prior to a desired execution. And, as a rule, if procedures are used recursively, the option "result" needs to be in the equation, too.

Sample program (declaration):

```
program call_recursive
implicit none
      integer :: m, n
      m = 10


      print *, ' it is defined that the factorial 10 has the
value'
      n = myfactorial (10)
      print *, n
end program call_recursive


! computation for factorial
recursive function factorial result (fac)
! result function
implicit none
```

6.5 – Understanding Internal Procedures

Internal procedures work similarly to external procedures. The difference with them, however, is that they contain internal functions.

Unlike their external counterparts, the declaration for the procedures merely requires you to specify that within the structure, there are executable statements. For example, when declaring internal procedures, a program would be written as follows:

```
program internal_procedures
implicit none
    ! type declaration
    ! executable statements


. . .

    contains
        ! internal procedures
. . .
end program internal_procedures
```

Sample program:

```
program internal_main
implicit none
real :: s, t
    s = 4.0
    t = 5.0
```

```fortran
    print *, 'Call before swap'
    print *, 's = ', s
    print *, 't = ', t

    call swap (s, t)
    print *, 'Call after swap'
    print *, 's = ', s
    print *, 't = ', t
contains
        internal swap (s, t)
            real :: s, t, temp
            temp = s
            s = t
            t = temp
        end internal swap
end program internal_main
```

Sample program (execution):

```
Call before swap
s = 4.0
t = 5.0

Call after swap
s = 5.0
t = 4.0
```

6.6 - Procedures & Arguments

Different discussions have emerged regarding procedures and arguments; the most common of which gives light to the question whether procedures can be written and used as arguments. Granted a function is defined in the statement and an actual argument exists, the answer is YES, PROCEDURES CAN BE CREATED AS ARGUMENTS.

Sample program:

```
program proc_arg
implicit none
    interface
        real function function (t)
            real intent :: t
        end real function function
    end interface

    call sub ( r, s, func (2) )
end program proc_arg
```

6.7 - Modules & Procedures

Although they are rather new to FORTRAN, modules are important to the programming language. They were introduced to contain heaps of elements such as data, procedures, and definitions. With them, the substantial portions that were written using the language are accessible to a programmer who is using another programming language.

Sample code:

```
program module_1
implicit none
    module module_1
        definitions


        ! contains modules and procedures
    end module module_1
end program module_1
```

6.8 - Public & Private Modules

Granted that the correct "use" statement is declared, a module can be accessible to all audiences. However, since open availability can herd in problem that can but a program in potential risk, it is recommended to restrict access and limit it to variable declaration, procedures, and statements.

Chapter 7: Manipulating Variable Amounts

Now let's do a little review of what has been learned so far. You have learned how to create a simple program in FORTRAN that inputs and outputs characters and numbers on the screen. You also have learned that there are operators that can do mathematical functions, and you can also display the results of those computations on the screen. You have also learned about variables and at least three different data types. Given all that you should be able to write a short program that manipulates variable amounts. In other words, you now know how to write a program in FORTRAN that can do some math.

Before we start making a program that can do simple arithmetic let's take a look a little closer at the details behind the operators first. The trick with operators is to not think of them as mathematical symbols. For instance when you see the statement

```
a = 2
```

It simply means that a value of 2 is stored in your computer's memory location that has been labeled as "a." Don't try to look at it as some sort of algebraic formula. In mathematics, "a" will be equal to 2, but that's not how it goes in FORTRAN or in any other programming language. Now let's take a look at a sequence of statements like this:

```
a = 2
b = 3
```

```
c = a + b
```

In the above sequence of statements, the value of 2 will be stored in your computer's memory location labeled as "a" and memory location "b" will store the value 3. Finally, memory location "c" will then add the values stored in both "a" and "b."

Remember that you can't write the code in this manner:

```
a + b = c
```

When the compiler goes through this line it will return an error. Note that there can only be one variable on the left hand side of the equal sign ("="). Some people forget that they are writing code and sometimes shift to writing math equations. Some mathematical rules are also applied in FORTRAN but not all of them. You should make it a point to learn all the coding conventions as you learn more about this and other programming languages.

7.1 - Arithmetic Operators

Not all math symbols will appear on your keyboard. It's also not possible to incorporate into code all the symbols in mathematics exactly as they appear. Since that is the case, FORTRAN makes use of its own symbols to represent certain math operands. Here are some of them that beginners should be aware of:

- + is for plus or addition
- - is for minus or subtraction

- * is for multiplication
- / is the symbol in FORTRAN for division
- ** is the symbol used for exponentiation
- () is used for brackets

Note that in FORTRAN the precedence of operands in mathematics is followed. However, you can also override the sequence of evaluating the math operations by using brackets. As you know, in algebra, when you see two variables side by side it denotes multiplication. That isn't possible in this programming language. FORTRAN compilers won't interpret it that way. You will still have to include the symbol for multiplication. That means coding it this way is wrong:

```
ab
```

If you want to multiply the value of "a" with that of "b" then you will have to code it like this:

```
a * b
```

Math operations are usually evaluated from left to right especially if the operators in question are of equal standing in their precedence. The evaluation of exponentiation is also done from left to right when there are consecutive exponentiations.

Here's a sample code that makes use of different arithmetic operators in FORTRAN:

```
program mysamplemath
```

```
implicit none

! this demonstrates how math operations work

real :: a, b, c, finalanswer

a= 2.6

b= 3.7

c= 4.8

finalanswer= a + b / c

print *,'and the answer is', finalanswer

end program mysamplemath
```

At this point you should take time to experiment with the different math operators available in FORTRAN. You can modify the code above to include different values. Use brackets to alter the sequence of the operations. You may even do the math yourself first and then write the code in FORTRAN and compare the results. That way you will have an idea how each of these operators work.

Make sure to use exponentiations as well. Remember to open new files for each change or alteration in the code that you make and make sure to change the program name each time you change something. That way you can trace what each code sequence will do. Doing these exercises will also help you practice providing logical sequences of statements or instructions.

7.2 - Blanks (Skip Positions)

Some novice programmers may wonder why blanks, sometimes called skip positions, are included in a program.

While there are others who insist on writing programs without them, most programmers prefer to incorporate these additional spaces to improve readability.

7.3 - Special Characters

In a program, special characters are used to deliver a function. Although they seem rather plain, you are advised to use them accordingly. If they are combined with each other, there may be conditions that dictate cancellation.

CHARACTER	DEFINITION
/	To specify another line
' '	To output strings
:	To terminate a list
( )	To categorize descriptors

7.5 – Descriptors

Descriptors, or better known as edit descriptors, are variables intended for specifying the amount of data required for conversion. It's recommended to keep track of their usage since processes may not end unless a succeeding descriptor is introduced.

LETTER	DEFINITION

FORTRAN Programming Success in a Day 2nd Edition

A	Repetition
D	Digits next to decimal points
E	Exponential number
M	Minimum digits
W	Width; total characters

Chapter 8: Intrinsic Functions in FORTRAN

You have now been introduced to some of the basic mathematical functions in FORTRAN. This programming language is truly at its best where mathematical computations are required. The following are the intrinsic functions that you can use.

- tan(x) – this function is used for tangent and it returns real numbers
- atan(x) – this function is used to compute arctangent and it also returns real numbers
- sin(x) – used for sine and it returns real numbers
- cos(x) – this function is used to denote cosine and it also returns real numbers
- abs(x) – this function is used to compute for the absolute value and it can return either real numbers or integers.
- sqrt(x) – is the function used for the square root of a number and it also returns a real number

You can use these intrinsic functions in your calculations. Of course, FORTRAN has a lot of functions and listing all of them in this book will be futile. However, given the functions provided in this list you practice making your code including different variables in your calculations. You should also note that trigonometric functions in FORTRAN are calculated in radians.

The following code demonstrates how sine is calculated where the user is supposed to enter any angle that is between 0 and 90 degrees.

```fortran
program testthefunk

!this program computes for sine

implicit none
    real :: x,y
    print *,'Please enter an  angle, It should be between
    0 degrees and 90 degrees'
    read *, x
    y = 4.0*atan(1.0)
    print *,'sine of ',x,'is',sin(x*y/180)
end program testthefunk
```

You may use other equations and tweak the code provided here. As usual you may also test the results of the equations and do the math yourself. If you want to learn the other functions that are available in FORTRAN you may consult a more exhaustive guide. Remember that this book is only meant to teach you the basics.

8.1 - What about Monte Carlo Simulations & Random Numbers?

In FORTRAN, Monte Carlo simulation describes the technique of picking out random (yet essential) data from a bunch. It argues that a basic presentation of data can go a long way; it can be used to alter the possible results or intervals of real numbers and integers.

The term "Monte Carlo" is associated in FORTRAN simulation since in the old days, particularly, back when computers were unheard of, the place Monte Carlo had a reputation as the go-to when it comes to obtaining data randomly. During the early years, many people gambled and the concept behind one of their effective money-making approaches was adopted in the programming language.

8.2 - The WRITE Line

Also called WRITE statements, WRITE lines are list-directed output. They can present the results of batches of expressions and strings. More importantly, they are declared to display an output on the screen.

What to remember about WRITE lines:

- In most cases, if their elements can't fit in a single line, the computer automatically proceeds their display onto the next line

- Their 2nd form does not contain any variable; instead they simply introduce a blank line

- They require a new line to start

Sample program:

```
program write_line
implicit none
    real :: destination
    integer :: time
    character ( len = 30 ), parameter :: 'The time to
reach your destination is'
```

```
    target :: 3.0
    destination ::4.0
    write *, 'target' = ', target
    write *, 'destination' = ', destination
end program write_line
```

Sample program (execution):

```
target = 3.0 (hours)
destination = 4.0 (kilometers)
```

```
The target time to reach your destination is 12.0 hours
```

8.3 - The READ Line

READ lines, also called READ statements, are list-directed data. As their name suggests, they can read through into a stack of input values, then, have them converted into variables that can be read even by non-programmers.

What to remember about READ lines:

- If they are presented with a list, they tend to skip a line
- If they need input values, a new line has to be introduced together with the input
- Their execution always begins by searching for input values and fresh input lines

- They can accommodate limited conversions

- They can appear on several lines

- They require a new line to start

Sample program:

```
program read_line
implicit none
     character ( len = 5 ) :: name1
     real :: school, height
     integer :: weight, eye color
read *, name1, school, height, weight, eye color
end program read_line
```

Sample program (execution; with sample input):

```
name1           "Dana Caulfield"
school     "Blackwell Academy"
height     "5 feet, 5 inches"
weight     "55 kilos"
eye color "almond"
```

Chapter 9: Conditional Statements

So far you have been introduced to mathematical operators as well as the intrinsic mathematical functions in FORTRAN. In this chapter you will be introduced to a different kind of operator – a logical operator. This is another reason why programming is such fun for many people. The codes that you have been exposed so far make your computer act like a calculator. However, it actually has a lot more computing power than that. Based on different conditions, your computer can also make decisions. This is where logical operators come into play. Note that all computer programming languages have conditional statements or conditional operators.

Consider the syntax of the sample statement below:

```
if (x == 1) then
print *, 'turn left'
end if
```

The logical operator "==" in this example are used in conjunction with the statements "if... then... end if" statements. Note the expression following the "if" statement. It provides a test, which is necessary when you are trying to imply a condition. In this case we can assume that the variable named "x" is an integer. One of its values can be equal to 1.

Interpreting this logical operation, the program is testing if the value of the variable is 1. The program will then check if this is true or not. If it is true then the statements in between the statements "then" and "end if" will be executed. In case the value of the variable "x" is not equal to 1 then the statement print *,'turn left' will not be executed.

Note that in the syntax of the statement if (<value> == <value>), there is no space in between the two equal signs in this logical operator. Putting a space in between these two equal signs will make any compiler return an error in the statement's syntax. The "end if" statement terminates the condition initiated by the "if" statement preceding it.

9.1 - Some Programming Conventions

The following is a bit of programming convention. It has no direct effect on how a compiler will translate your code. Take a look at how the previous code is written below:

```
if  (x == 1) then
     print *,'turn left'
     !do you notice anything
end if
```

Well, other than the comment line that was added, you will also notice that the statements in between the 'if' statement and the 'end if' statement have been indented. Yes, even the comment was indented as well. This is another programming convention or practice. It's pretty common in many programming languages including the ones that make use of a top down design.

Making these indentations make the code more readable to a human being. By that you will know that the indented statements are somewhat embedded within the 'if...' – 'end if statement.'

You have already been introduced to other programming conventions earlier in this book. For instance, you have been encoding the statement 'implicit none' when dealing with variables and you even place it at the very beginning of your code. You have also been instructed that comments should be helpful to the reader of your code. The variable names that you choose in your code should make sense and be meaningful. The prompts that you display on the screen should help the user figure out what types of data is expected as input. Remember that making your program work isn't the only important thing in programming, especially in FORTRAN. The way you code also speaks a lot about how well versed you are as a programmer. These conventions have been proven to make the work of coding and troubleshooting code a lot easier.

9.2 - Solving Logical Problems with Logic Operators

You can actually write a series of logical operators to help the program figure out what action it is to take next. In the examples that have been provided in this book, a huge portion of the success of these logic operators depends on the user and his ability to input the correct response. Most of the time, you will give the user several options on the screen. Unfortunately, it doesn't matter how well you have crafted the prompts in your code, some users still enter the wrong type of data. They may also enter a value that isn't one of the options you have indicated in your prompts.

To solve this dilemma, you may craft your if-then statements this way:

```
if  (userinput == 1) then
     <the program will execute certain set of statements>
     else if  (userinput == 2) then
     <the program will execute certain set of statements>
     else
     <execute   these   statements   if   the   user   entered
something else>
end if
```

This statement is actually a new structure in FORTRAN. This statement makes use of '*if-else-end if*' to cancel out the possibility that the user will enter anything else other than the desired result. This is also especially useful when you want to be able to control the next statements that will be executed when equations may provide different results.

Another bit of info that you should also know is that you can embed conditional statements within conditional statements. You can do that to test for a specific value or a specific type of condition. Just make sure that you arrange the code with proper indentation or else you some of your if-statements will not have either an else-if or else-statement to pair with it. Your compiler will definitely return an error when such a mistake in syntax occurs.

9.3 - More Logical Operators

Of course there are more logical operators in FORTRAN other than the "==" or test for equality. The following are the other logical operators that you can use when crafting your codes:

not equal to	/=
less than	<
greater than	>
greater than or equal to	>=
less than/equal to	<=

Here is a sample code using different logical operators. This one actually makes use of multiple conditions where one conditional statement is embedded in another:

```
if  (a > b) then
    if  (x <= y) then
        <perform these statements>
    end if
end if
```

Another construct that you can use in logical operations is ".and." which you can use to satisfy different conditions. Consider the following example:

```
if  (a == b .and. c < d) then
    <perform these statements>
```

```
end if
```

Conclusion

Thank you again for purchasing this book!

I hope this book was able to help you to understand the basics in FORTRAN programming.

The next step is to practice the codes and make your first few programs. You should also test them and troubleshoot potential issues that may arise using your compiler.

Finally, if you enjoyed this book, please take the time to share your thoughts and post a review on Amazon. It'd be greatly appreciated!

Thank you and good luck!

Check Out My Other Books

Below you'll find some of my other popular books that are popular on Amazon and Kindle as well. Simply click on the links below to check them out. Alternatively, you can visit my author page on Amazon to see other work done by me.

Android Programming in a Day

Python Programming in a Day

C Programming Success in a Day

C Programming Professional Made Easy

JavaScript Programming Made Easy

PHP Programming Professional Made Easy

C ++ Programming Success in a Day

Windows 8 Tips for Beginners

HTML Professional Programming Made Easy

31802883R00049

Printed in Poland
by Amazon Fulfillment
Poland Sp. z o.o., Wrocław